MY FAULT

RECENT TITLES FROM THE CLEVELAND STATE UNIVERSITY POETRY CENTER

The Hartford Book by Samuel Amadon
Rust or Go Missing by Lily Brown
The Grief Performance by Emily Kendal Frey
Stop Wanting by Lizzie Harris
Vow by Rebecca Hazelton
The Tulip-Flame by Chloe Honum
Render / An Apocalypse by Rebecca Gayle Howell
A Boot's a Boot by Lesle Lewis
Say So by Dora Malech
50 Water Dreams by Siwar Masannat
Mule by Shane McCrae
Festival by Broc Rossell
The Firestorm by Zach Savich
Mother Was a Tragic Girl by Sandra Simonds
I Live in a Hut by S.E. Smith
I Burned at the Feast: Selected Poems of Arseny Tarkovsky translated by Philip Metres
    and Dimitri Psurtsev
Bottle the Bottles the Bottles the Bottles by Lee Upton
Adventures in the Lost Interiors of America by William D. Waltz
Uncanny Valley by Jon Woodward
You Are Not Dead by Wendy Xu

For a complete list of titles please visit
www.csupoetrycenter.com

MY FAULT

LEORA FRIDMAN

Cleveland State University Poetry Center
Cleveland, Ohio

ISBN 978-0-9963167-1-2

First edition

20   19   18   17   16   5   4   3   2   1

This book is published by the Cleveland State University Poetry Center,
2121 Euclid Avenue, Cleveland, Ohio 44115-2214
www.csupoetrycenter.com and is distributed by
SPD / Small Press Distribution, Inc. www.spdbooks.org.

Cover image: Anna Hepler (www.annahepler.com)
My Fault was designed and typeset by Amy Freels in Stone Print with Sertig display.

A catalog record for this title is available from the Library of Congress.

for Mom, Papi and Gabi, who brought me this life and founded my weird language

Pained and similar plants, now don't I have to give?
—Alice Notley

CONTENTS

1

2

3

4

1

GROWN TO COVET

I am the most myself when watching
a stranger hit my hand

I am the most rested
when I hate on this land

I am the most accepting
but no town wants to agree

to accept a mucking
in our very clean sea

because clean is also a venture
a good delivery man

because too much comprehension
is also a demand

my fault has grown these days
so many lumps in one place

I have grown to covet
a more committed race

I have grown to covet
skin tilting on a place

this is why we all
are humbled by a face

PROVING A BIRD

My body
is no wild
thing:

I speak,
surrender,

am mean
to strange men.

What walk
protects me

on a grey
street?

Am I
to mumble?

Am I
to beg?

Proving a bird,
I play lamely

at the feet
of the sun.

I call upon
giants.

HOW TO HOLD

The first way is briefly
knowing someone
who does not drive
but moves about the city
so quickly you have
gripping jealous pangs
while you watch
their day elapse.
You are getting to know
them slowly and try
to deliver acceptance
into the instants
you are together.
At the gym you
and the person grab
very different objects.
Your object is one
you could lift and steal
easily without much regret.
You normally feel regret
and are proud of
your ethics, but
when it comes to things
you can easily cover
with only your hands
you do not defend

them from yourself.
The second way
is not waiting, and
seizing, instead,
onto their capable hands.

TO THE RECENT SEA

I say lift me:
I am a motherfucking load.

The more people come to understand
the more
they love
my sister.

A grey
kind of family
this is:

flush like ancient
Rome.

Level with the
hyper kids.

Please.

Do you know love
when love hops
gladly?

When love
moves?

Can you tell me
what an arcade
means?

No meaning
is patient
with me.

Each gift
I bring with

floods
overnight.

RIGOR

You are inspiring
the way inspiring works
for me: you are also
reverent, the way
that reverent can see
how any burgeoning
plant life will never
care about my tone,
how any shoots
meant for eating
will fear what else
is sown, how each cover
I place over privates
is a system
I designed,
how keeping it on
makes me respectful,
and keeping it meek
isn't shown

WICKED ALMOST

If we keep at it like this,
we'll never eat.

Triumphant gizzards
& influential men:

we remain unable
to curtail ourselves.

We'll blow out flares of chitlins &
dependencies on flight.

We'll talk across eons of want.

Every light is a skitterer.

Those shards
that become globules
when you stare them down.

We win at things by ignoring.

We reach out for distribution,
almost like we wanted to meet.

TOO WILLING

I get wrapt
by a group
of plants
grown still
in the cold, or

is that how
growth goes,
does everyone know
how to view
this event
already

*

I have an idea
my captain
is my skin

press uneven against me
like a real body could

there is
no even
evolution

*

am I
too willing

to be safe
on legs?

when
I want every

body
to speak

WHAT YOU KEEP IN YOUR BLOUSE

I have not shot
a single animal

I have not met
the governing body

I have not called
them directly

I have not leaned
in far to see, but

since I got here
I've been yelling

running alongside
in the direction

of all feats
I can view

*

there is no alarm
for this sleeping

but this is the softness
I naturally grow:

I promised my mother
each breath would remind me

the way I move
is I move with meetings

I try to stay within
all these asks

try to remember I'm a party
who can participate

& envoys
have come before me

with alternatives
to disengagement

how they pushed key players
into the ring

how they didn't force
anyone to fight

saying *you can hold
yourself back*

*

what I'm seeking
is gatherings

where I can easily
deliver my mind

especially on the days
when I run lax, laxly,

especially on the days
my blind eye pours:

people say these
are essential procedures

don't keep them to
yourself this morning, or

the way you're moving
may stay just yours

WHICH SNOWSTORM IS STILL ALIVE

the neighborhood
does not wonder.

It is still winter
among poplars and pines.

We have less belief
to maintain.

Under cover of misfortune
I go plowing through noise,

I go lifting everything
but my arms.

Which snowstorm
can hear me.

Which human
alights.

I am nobody
but listening,

some unexplained
wife.

READY TO TELL YOU

I have recycled the calling
I thought that I had
this is one way to have a family
this is another way to decant
one trial into the next starter
how to experiment exquisitely
how to clean my uncertain spore
just you try pulling yesterday's proof
into hymns about present day
this is not the way we preserve us or
the precious coast we could restore

2

3D HOUSE OF BEEF

This is me at the table with my three friends. Actually it's no friends, it's animals I said I would eat. Hello, obligation to be free. Hello, every last friend I didn't make. I'm giving up on you. I am going to stand only on the things I feel like standing on, and sometimes that means they have a little sinkhole. Sometimes I'll sink a little into this 3D House of Beef. At least my slope's made of something. You don't even have a hand. You don't even have a hand in making a home for yourself. I don't blame you, but I stand on my beef. When I stand in here I can make my table out of anything and I don't have to explain. This is an animal I'm standing on and I know what being that means. These are houses of allegiance. These rooms are familiar slides. If a friend wants to come over they have to deal with the beef first. They might try to be outraged at the beef, but that will only make them slide faster. These slopes are friendly. You can see them again if you want. You can talk human to these slopes. I'll stand on my extroverted slopes and they'll stand in for me.

DELICATE MATTERS

I said
don't mind me

impressing this
upon you

I feed you
safely

my hurting
turf

my conscientious
waste

meals as protectors
of broke chemistry

every ache sound
we can't eat

becomes a cheap
solution

becomes mild fodder
for play

*

we play
because it matters

recreation
for relief

how could you
lessen levels

if you never
ever shame

*

the curse
will find us shortly

on the planet
we have grown

what matters
spares us

what matters
goes to seed

*

I can be your
levelheaded leader

manufactured
deep inside

a balmy
reprieve

I can express less
from what we eat

press the most
delicate shapes

out through
a glaring sieve

STORAGE

I am a cubby
for wanting

you too
can see

every anthem on the ocean
is unfairly elegant

I pride myself
on not being convinced

*

the fisheries deny me

my fly   droops

do you have enough flesh
for all of us

would you like me
to put it away

LABOR

I prefer it when, like a factory stripped,
no one goes to bed like they are supposed to.
This is the drive I make every day in the dark:
a child strapped to a tree trunk, calling, please
don't commute to me. Please don't drive with
bellies filled with your rights. I have liberty enough,
a linear attention to the call of the wild, in which
everyone I'm not seeing gets belted and searched
by someone else. I asked no one to search so invasively,
but these, young lady, are the days we have been given.
We must not get side-swiped by more assertive men.
When you are resting I hope you imagine the walls of
manufacturing buildings falling away from you
as you tour the factory where suffering young ladies
once made yarn. It's not in fashion to wear that cloth
to work now, though it is always in fashion to tour factories
of other times. While you sleep more children keep working,
more people who don't call out from the wilderness because
they have no desire for wilderness in the way you visit
it now. You are able to focus on action when you stare
at a single cheek. You claim a candy striper supervised you
in a job you worked from home.

INDOOR POEM

I have a hyacinth
in the garden of my dreams,
where no one is drooling
over anything.

Inside the hyacinth
bees can live
but can't come out.

They have everything they need in there.

I'm not proud of them.

We are only drilling
toward a sculpted place.

We are only looking about.

Who can say where the handle is
to make this an opening door?

Who can hit
my switch?

I am no laughing hyacinth
surrounded by gold.

I am no contrast
glittering with seed.

Every chair compels me.

Every culture
has its decorative arts.

FAULT

we all keep on walking
so that we can look small

we preserve seaweed
sustain an easy lore

believing in our touches
living lightly on the land

by raising populations
proclaimed innocent on one score

*

every person stands yelling
at any kiss of death

no fault is our fault
just fractures in the land

when raising populations
who build under their breath

a pillar is for finding
what doesn't make it fall

*

what's at the top of no trees
pressing into no sky

a well-lit vista
regal and banal

gas stations stop us
make us want to hide

by raising populations
proclaimed innocent on one score

we preserve seaweed
sustain an easy lore

we do not notice neon
signs that thunk ashore

BRED

I press on you falsely

cushioned
falsely

a body bred
for consoling mouths

I am pending   you

I tire easily,
I explain,

a good bird
takes the call

FOOL'S ERRAND

Such an undertaking
as you have taken
is my silent light:

I believe you
because you progress,
because you
don't remain.

Have you
explained
yourself?

Every new friend
I made in December
was right.

They knew my love.

They knew the winter
would recline.

Between all of us
we generate jobs.

We have enough work
to leap over
any frozen lake,

never fall below
suspended.

Call me
a day of rest.

Call me your
modern girlfriend
who gets with
the times.

When anyone
presses flowers
I check the date:

how many names
can there truly be
for this, our era
in time.

3

POEM FOR CARRIE LORIG
AND RAÚL ZURITA

When I heard
the first bang

I thought
any scream

rips my ribcage
like a shaming caress.

My body is
a common place,

something alive,
not an occasion.

Now everything
moves, more

fine than a
fine girl petting

the neighborhood
rat. Now I know

it: the girl
nods instead

of screaming.

LECTURE

I accept some omissions

from the man who wrote me twice

claiming he loves me for

my body parts like apples

not sweet or stable

not accurate or brief

I have come to withstand him

and believe that any praying

can be treated as a fight

for the body I love lately

the eyebrows run amuck

the careful stomach

behaving tonight

behaving so manly

that I can barely hear

who else is talking

explaining how we fear

MY DISPERSING SORRY

my new pledge
is I will matter

without
being fuel

today goodbyes
are gas station buzz

used up like coaxing
which turns me off slowly

as if I am unavailable
but available for freight

thinking now of how much more
people find me exciting

when I am not dumped with light
when large flat forces

are denying me something
more significant

than steak
when judging by your face

I am no middle America,
no quietly crucial selection

that remains to be made
between what rules us

instead just a flatlands
an optimized place

not calling for a vision
or a game that relates

but every atmosphere flying over
can't carry much more, just

looks down on us sunning
so promising from above

looks down on us guaranteeing
as we forget one more pledge

TAKE THE CALL

when requested

I grow weary

can you answer

my wants

can any gap

be foodie

embodied

is this

excess

is this

hating

can any explanation

dispel

FACTIONS

a good joke is calling
my friend up & saying
I have not found
any skin yet but I will
be there soon, just as
soon as I can fight off
the beavers peeling fibers
from my scalp, trying
to open my mind,
making me feel far
more awake than
I ever intended to find
myself, laughing at
how much human I am,
how pressed I am to this
place: this is what I
intended to say when
I crept so easily up to a tree
because this is no random
estrangement, this is
the speech we have bred

AWNING

I've roped myself
out of another one.

I've left my favorite dress behind.
The way we move from crash to crash

is like springing beasts, and I can't take
credit for the forward march.

I allow myself this gravity
because I think it makes others

feel welcome. You know, we can't always
be discussing our latest greatest find.

Down by the old accident there are those
nice people without hope. They can spell

out everything they're feeling
without the help of poise.

They can see until the river bends.
We like one another when I am

piecing my dress back together.
They feel my pain.

They know what it is like to keep stitching
in the name of dumb faith.

That always renewing stoppage.
That falling on top of what's next,

blocking its boring vegetable
fame. Nobody thinks

they are going to get anywhere,
just the pure blank doing,

a floating marquee
on the stream.

PITY

I am some grounded
religion

I am some answer
no one told

meaning also
I make a living

I explain
the best caress

like what obvious metals
does the earth most need

and which ones can we leave
praying for ourselves

BECAUSE IT WAS AN INCIDENT

I dialed out for help. People came over
and were quiet around their mouths.
People busied themselves shelling snap
peas that I had not anticipated would come in
so soon. People brought with them stories of
the sights. They had stood on ice floes in order
to watch the decay and had learned to leap higher
than the mines. I expected this superhuman
behavior given how incapacitated I found myself.
More people went out for filo dough as if only
to mock me, not to eat. As if a flight to the Balkans
was what put a planet over the edge. As if talking
wasn't moving. *Don't stand by the window,*
someone told me, *you might be mistaken for
a virtual face.* The house was full of pictures
of how to make a mild scene.

CULTIVATION

Living above land
is my new failure:

there is no lover who
could trust me this way

I march for satisfaction
& pull right my boots

this is definitely how I pray, I mean,
calling up laws of nature

yelling, *don't plant here*

gripping on the sandy ground, saying,
how many more things could be grown

here in a shifting dirt,
it has been used

so many —
or not yelling

out of wanting
to leave no trace

*

I reprimand these plants for staying
the way they never should have held

we know every thing is dying,
roots warped by sandy soil,

we know our holdings have
a history of unsafety,

someone owned them so wholly,
someone acted on their behalf

that way *we people*
know it's risky to own land:

my father said, *we are frightened of real estate,*
it's what they can take from us

we buy only what we can move
we trade in caution

& when I see my ancestors walk
it's on a road you can't sink in

it's a road that allows you
to leave without speaking

without telling anyone
an Irish goodbye,

ghosting from whence you came,
no sacred failures at your back

because you are not a grower
or any other personnel

you are never heard talking
without caution

you are never heard whistling
bare odes, indiscreet

*

I call this my cultivation,
what I prefer to heed:

every flux
every weather

is a reason
to away

the reason that states humbly
the reason that lulls

lulls all of me
into business

the business of driving
from one trait to the next

inheriting bad news,
an evolved way to shelter —

some call it farming
on the mutable home

4

CAN WE SHARE THE PLEASURES

after Saint Teresa of Ávila

It is now my belief
that we made a playdate

no two people are sure

yet I do not suppose we have any need
for people who are sure

when you live among them
you imitate

no true people
gain notoriety

but I name no names

my urge, too,
must needs have happened

yet I did not suppose a systematic mode
would come looking

this is what I've tried to show in my work

there are noises in the audience of appreciation
so I am afraid

that, at least, is what I am afraid of
that everything I say may be confused

that, even, may be it entire

that may be why   we say

I am afraid of noises with which
I may be confused

seeing how we bare absence
we imitate, sure

it doesn't appear   a system is coming

no two people are sure
what I've tried to show

but it's my urge, too

notoriety is merely knowing someone
& their supposed name

at the very least people are sure
about working

two people are afraid   they may really be looking to live

the more you can tell the more you can
live among –

      not to know what channel's on
      but always to be pleading, as in:

what criteria put mama
on a bender

or:

deep in the craft store a woman gets angry
      dials back her sure noise

she's not crocheting for urges,
nor is she lying low

she's exiting premises
yet another made

channeling no mother,
reaching to embrace

      this is where the bodies go
      in winter, where
      the perils get sown

      by & large I can tell
      where the fabric pulled

more people wanting   a more spacious face

billions bent down   to be level

lapsed into   what went well
in tests of waste

no one has a handle
for this toilet bowl

sure as her buttons
the noise will increase

each tries to show wisdom in her work
I take a bow for all

wisdom pulls the handle
ordinarily when we meet

the ordinary criteria
work the room

each guest visits
insists on staying nearby

I'm not trying to watch over
but she rooms around this place

this hour is my exit
this noise is me attempting

to show someone
how to leave

when you live among them
you do not suppose

you will rise rigid with certainty

all play is sure here
for notorious gain

few of us are absent
at the urge to be afraid

suppose any need
could come looking

suppose anyone who wanted
could be prepared

suppose everything I say
could come confused to call

could show any audience
how my needs mimic them

at the very least people are
now merely my belief

what more can you touch today
with a winter so wet

in terms well told now
a gentleman calls

deep inside the craft store
he does not hear any "no"s

he hears everyone chatting
about their greatest fear

on a level he is with us
looking us over all the time

we present ourselves pleading
tall and mother-made

the same man encounters
wells dug level to the street

and asks who will measure
once the flush is gone

the man test-buys a liquid
to turn us face-up

for all of our desiring
more want to be chaste

when two go to bed all
rise again

this is the rhythm
of the tight

when two bodies look at each other
criteria arise

surely two more tenants
won't show the Bill of Rights

won't decide
what we can host

how not rising
begins to diagnose

more people drive
across the dark to show

appallingly proud
to dial their mothers
with news

about every talk
they are given

every late night
risk aversion

every careful speech
they've been read

one criteria
of a good wisdom:

keep rigid what
you said

two more tenants showed faces
and brought updates to friends

a development clearly
good to one another

down with people
more driven

you can fluff
or no show

have you gardened night-bloomers
faces that just grow

who faces up to vagueness
after clear comes home

or up-keep is easy
when belief cups the hand

conviction is easy
flying over this land

the identity of mother
came blatant to my heart

I can't afford it, explanation
goes black

the gaps we worship
fall happily at our feet

I'm drawing more comfort
from far-away prices

drawing more comfort
from being alone

each mom we walked by
sounded an alert

people's sounds protesting
small cuttings they made

without any caressing
I could scope the entire

walk back from the lake
fail to describe us

we meet to believe and
the breach points me home

I suppose the consternation
is a cutting in itself

my speaking repulses
my belief walks

these bulbs are me pulling
my swath through loam

these bulbs are me strolling
lighting myself home

your job was to call me
remind me to appear

with dismay I arrived here
found no fair we could attend

can we share the pleasures
I feel when you suspend

while everyone argued
I contented myself

with quietly judging
what was enough mess

we are still growing
our names on the stem

we are still riding
authentically in place

I suppose the consternation
is a cutting in itself

I went for the blaming
& found there more embrace

ACKNOWLEDGMENTS

So many people have made it possible for me to arise and quake and arise again with these poems.

Thank you to all the editors who have supported this work, including the editors at *Drunken Boat, Timber, Powder Keg, Banango Street, Sixth Finch, The Atlas Review, Noö Journal, epiphany, The Bakery,* and *The Awl.* Poems in this collection were included in the chapbook *Obvious Metals* from Projective Industries, and in the chapbook *Precious Coast* from H_NGM_N. Thank you Nate Pritts and Stephanie Anderson for believing in books.

Other people's words make it possible for me to make: the title "3D House of Beef" is from Peter Gizzi, "Proving a Bird" is from Sarah Green, "Because It Was an Incident" is from Rosamond Purcell, "Grown to Covet" and "What You Keep in Your Blouse" are from Nick Sturm, and "Ready to Tell You" is from Wendy Xu.

I am grateful forever to my teachers, Dara Wier, Peter Gizzi, Lisa Olstein, James Tate (z"l), Forrest Gander, Jibade Khalil Huffman, Connie Biewald, Phyllis Kutt (z"l), Joanie Grisham, and everyone all the way back who let me read when I wanted to and asked me to try hard.

Thank you Eileen Myles and Caryl Pagel and everyone at CSU for making this.

Thank you and muchichísimas gracias to my family, Mom, Papi and Gabi, for making it possible for me to swallow books and speak strangely and make up worlds. Thank you to my grandparents, Abuelita, Luis (z"l), Grandma Ruth (z"l) and Grandpa Lester (z"l), for the imaginations and the history that allows me to speak. Thank you Charlene and Sam and Leah for accepting a poet into your family so wholeheartedly.

Thank you to my friends / the quake-hearts who've made writing possible for me: Kelin Loe, Ellie Lobovits, Liat Berdugo, Joanna Roberts, Cailey Gibson, Wendy Xu, Carrie Lorig, Sarah Green, Sunisa Manning, Tess Lantos, Megan Brattain, Katie Loncke, Stefanie Simons, Jon Corcoran, Adam Roberts, Abrah Dresdale, and everyone who lets me love them. For understanding, and for not having to understand every piece, but walking together.

Beyond the edges of this planet, thank you to Josh, my teammate for joy.

Photo: Ellie Lobovits

Leora Silverman Fridman is the author of the chapbooks *Precious Coast* (H_NGM_N Books), *Obvious Metals* (Projective Industries), *On the Architecture* and *Essential Nature* (The New Megaphone), and the chapbook of translations, *Eduardo Milán: Poems* (Toad Press). She lives in the San Francisco Bay Area, where she is founding co-editor of *Spoke Too Soon: A Journal of the Longer* and forms one fourth of the collective The Bureau.